Jane Addams

by Lucia Raatma

Compass Point Early Biographies

Content Adviser: Allen F. Davis, Jane Addams biographer,
Temple University,
Philadelphia, Pennsylvania

Reading Adviser: Dr. Linda D. Labbo,
Department of Reading Education, College of Education,
The University of Georgia

COMPASS POINT BOOKS
Minneapolis, Minnesota

Compass Point Books
3109 West 50th Street, #115
Minneapolis, MN 55410

Visit Compass Point Books on the Internet at *www.compasspointbooks.com*
or e-mail your request to *custserv@compasspointbooks.com*

Editor: Christianne C. Jones
Photo Researcher: Marcie C. Spence
Designer/Page Production: Bradfordesign, Inc./Les Tranby

Library of Congress Cataloging-in-Publication Data
Raatma, Lucia.
    Jane Addams / by Lucia Raatma.
        p. cm. — (Compass Point early biographies)
Summary: A brief biography of Jane Addams, who established Hull-House in Chicago in 1889
to provide medical and legal services, educational opportunities, and social interactions to
immigrants and other victims of poverty.
ISBN 0-7565-0566-6 (hardcover)
1. Addams, Jane, 1860-1935—Juvenile literature. 2. Women social workers—United
    States—Biography—Juvenile literature. 3. Women social reformers—United States—
    Biography—Juvenile literature. [1. Addams, Jane, 1860-1935. 2. Social workers.
    3. Women—Biography. 4. Nobel Prizes—Biography.] I. Title. II. Series.
HV28.A35R32 2004
361.92—dc22   2003012274

Table of Contents

*NOTE: In this book, words that are defined in the glossary
are in **bold** the first time they appear in the text.*

Giving to Others

Jane Addams lived her life to help others. In 1889, Jane and her friend Ellen Starr founded Hull-House in a poor section of Chicago, Illinois. This home offered services to less fortunate people, including people who didn't have jobs or homes. Jane helped improve working conditions for all people, especially women and children.

Another mission Jane strongly believed in was promoting world peace. For her work, Jane Addams was the first American woman to receive the Nobel Peace Prize.

◄ Jane Addams around 1910

A Comfortable Childhood

Jane Addams was born in the small town of Cedarville, Illinois, on September 6, 1860. Her father, John, was a wealthy businessman and a **political** leader.

Her mother died when Jane was only 2 years old. Jane became very attached to her father. When Jane was 7, her father married Anna H. Haldeman.

Jane's mother, Sarah Weber, around 1860

Jane learned a lot from her father. He taught her the importance of working hard and always doing her best. He explained to her at an early age that not everyone was as

John Addams and Anna H. Haldeman, Jane's stepmother, in 1868

lucky as they were. Jane knew it was important to help less fortunate people.

As a child, Jane had an illness that caused her spine to curve slightly. This was very painful for her. However, Jane did not let

Jane was a serious child who worked hard in school.

the problem keep her from having a normal childhood. Jane's father encouraged his daughter to get a good education and go to college. He also encouraged her to marry and have children. During Jane's childhood, few women worked outside the home. Being a wife and mother was a full-time job for most women.

A Strong-Minded Young Woman

In 1877, Jane Addams enrolled at the Rockford Female Seminary. She did well in her studies and graduated at the top of her class. She was a strong leader, and her classmates looked up to her.

After finishing at Rockford in 1881, Jane wanted to study medicine. Her family was

Jane Addams in 1878

The Women's Medical College of Pennsylvania was founded in 1850.

shocked by this idea! They worried that she would not marry. Jane saw her brothers working in science and medicine. She wanted to follow that same path. Having children and keeping a household did not appeal to her.

After her father's death in 1881, Jane pursued her dream and entered the Women's

The Women's Medical College of Pennsylvania was the first school to offer medical courses to women. ➤

Medical College of Pennsylvania. She missed her father terribly. Also, her back pain got much worse. Sometimes it hurt just to walk. Jane left school and had surgery to correct her back problem. After the operation, she was strapped into a back brace for almost an entire year!

A Trip to London

When Jane's health got better, she traveled to London with some friends, including college classmate Ellen Starr.

While in London, Jane and Ellen visited

Samuel and Henrietta Barnett founded Toynbee Hall.

Toynbee Hall. It was a **settlement house** founded in 1884. Toynbee Hall offered classes

and help to less
fortunate people.

Once Jane
was back in the
United States,
she couldn't
stop thinking
about Toynbee
Hall and the work
done there. Jane and

Ellen talked about the

Ellen Starr around 1880

need for a settlement
house in the United States. Before long,
the two young women decided to start
their own settlement house.

Founding Hull-House

In 1889, Jane and Ellen moved into an old house in a poor section of Chicago. They fixed it up and turned it into a settlement house. The two women called it Hull-House, after Charles Hull who had built it. Hull-House was used to improve the lives of people in the neighborhood.

Children enjoyed playing, reading, and learning at Hull-House.

Jane talked to many different people about the settlement house. She explained the need to help others. Within a few years, Hull-House offered medical care and legal services. Kindergarten classes and meetings were held there. At the house, **immigrants**

◄ One of the first buildings that was added to the original Hull-House included a coffee house and a gymnasium.

could learn to speak English and adjust to life in the United States. Hull-House also provided classes in music, art, and drama.

Mary Rozet Smith was one of the many women who worked with Jane and Ellen at the settlement house. Mary supported Hull-House and enjoyed helping. She and Jane became lifelong friends.

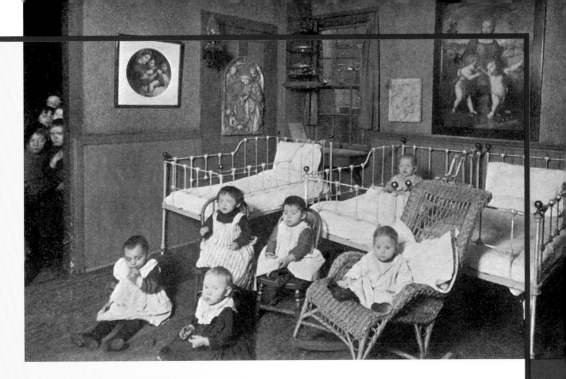

An important room in Hull-House was the nursery.

By 1893, Hull-House was helping more than 2,000 people a week! During this time, the United States was in the midst of a **depression.** Throughout the country, **poverty** was increasing. The work done at Hull-House became even more important.

◄ Mary Rozet Smith (left) and Jane Addams around 1896

Changing the Law

Jane Addams spoke out about improving the lives of factory workers. She saw people working in terrible conditions in dangerous factories. Jane worked with Julia Lathrop and Dr. Alice Hamilton to make changes. They helped pass new laws to protect factory workers.

Jane also heard about children working in these factories. The three women worked for better child labor laws.

Julia Lathrop

Dr. Alice Hamilton

Many children worked long hours in factories under strict supervision. They often had to skip school to work. ➤

Some factory owners did not like what Jane was saying. Horrible working conditions led to strikes and protests. Many people blamed Jane for the trouble. Some people stopped giving money to Hull-House.

Jane Addams traveled all over the world sharing her ideas about world peace, woman suffrage, and equal rights for everyone.

Jane began making extra money by giving speeches and writing articles about her ideas. She became quite well known. She wrote a number of books, including "Twenty Years at Hull-House." The book was the story of her life. It was published in 1910.

Helping Women and Promoting Peace

Jane also worked for woman **suffrage.** She believed that women should have the same rights as men. In 1911, she became first vice president of the National American Woman Suffrage Association.

A banner advertises a speech Jane Addams was to give at Carnegie Hall in New York in 1913.

In 1915, Addams organized the Women's Peace Party. She hoped that the work of this group would end World War I (1914–1918).

Once again, many people did not like what Jane had to say. She didn't let that bother her, though. She continued to work for peace, even in time of war. The Women's International League for Peace and Freedom was formed in 1919. Jane was the first president of the organization.

Jane Addams (middle) and other members of the Women's Peace Party arrive in Chicago before leaving for an International Peace Conference.

Members of the International Conference of Women for a Permanent Peace gathered in the Netherlands to promote peace in 1915.

Jane also helped begin other important organizations. In 1909, she helped start the National Association for the Advancement of Colored People (NAACP). The NAACP works for equal rights for African-Americans. In 1920, she helped start the American Civil Liberties Union (ACLU). The ACLU was created to promote freedom of speech.

During Jane's lifetime, the NAACP and the ACLU were seen as trouble-makers. Jane was criticized for her efforts. She had ideas that were different from other people's. Some people were frightened by her ideas. They said she was not a good American.

Jane Addams (right) and Mary McDowell stood strong in their beliefs to promote world peace.

A Life Remembered

No matter what people said about Jane Addams, Hull-House continued to be successful. In the 1930s, the United States suffered from the Great Depression. During this time, President Franklin Roosevelt agreed with many of Jane's ideas. In fact, he used some of her ideas to create

Children always played an important role in Jane's life.

government programs that helped people. Suddenly, Jane's views became more accepted throughout the world. She received many awards during this time.

In 1926, Jane had suffered a heart attack. She never fully recovered, and her health continued to get worse. Jane was admitted to the hospital on the same day the Nobel Peace Prize was being awarded to her in 1931.

She was able to work until she died in Chicago on May 21, 1935. Thousands of people came to her funeral at Hull-House.

Jane Addams spent her life helping others. She will always be remembered for her giving ways.

Jane Addams waiting to begin ➤
a radio broadcast in 1932

Important Dates in Jane Addams's Life

1860	Born on September 6 in Cedarville, Illinois
1877	Enrolls at Rockford Female Seminary
1881	Graduates from Rockford Female Seminary; enters Women's Medical College of Pennsylvania
1888	Tours Europe and visits Toynbee Hall in London
1889	Starts Hull-House in Chicago with Ellen Starr
1909	Helps start the NAACP
1910	Publishes "Twenty Years at Hull-House"
1911	Becomes the first vice president of the National American Woman Suffrage Association
1915	Helps create the Women's Peace Party
1919	Helps start the Women's International League for Peace and Freedom
1920	Helps start the ACLU
1931	Awarded the Nobel Peace Prize
1935	Dies on May 21 in Chicago at age 74

Glossary

depression—a time when businesses do badly and many people become poor

immigrants—people who move from one country to settle and live in another

political—dealing with the business of government, politics, or the state

poverty—the state of being poor

settlement house—a center set up to serve people in a poor neighborhood

suffrage—the right to vote

Did You Know?

- In 1910, Jane Addams received the first honorary degree given to a woman from Yale University.

- In 1895, Addams was appointed garbage inspector for a poor section of Chicago. She earned $1,000 a year. It was the only paying job she ever held.

- Hull-House established the first public playground, the first public swimming pool, and the first Boy Scout troop in Chicago.

- Hull-House was torn down in 1963. It was rebuilt and opened as a museum in 1967.

Want to Know More?

At the Library
Armentrout, David. *Jane Addams*. Vero Beach, Fla.: Rourke, 2002.

Edge, Laura Bufano. *A Personal Tour of Hull-House*. Minneapolis: Lerner, 2001.

Polikoff, Barbara Garland. *With One Bold Act: The Story of Jane Addams*.
    Chicago: Boswell Books, 1999.

Simon, Charnan. *Jane Addams: Pioneer Social Worker.* New York:
    Children's Press, 1997.

On the Web
For more information on *Jane Addams,* use FactHound
to track down Web sites related to this book.

   1. Go to *www.compasspointbooks.com/facthound*
   2. Type in this book ID: 0756505666
   3. Click on the *Fetch It* button.

Your trusty FactHound will fetch the best Web sites for you!

Through the Mail
Jane Addams Hull-House Association

Central Office

10 S. Riverside Plaza, Suite 1700

Chicago, IL 60606

For more information about the work of this organization

On the Road
Jane Addams Hull-House Museum

The University of Illinois at Chicago

800 S. Halsted St.

Chicago, IL 60607

To visit the museum and take a tour of Hull-House

Index

About the Author

Lucia Raatma received her bachelor's degree in English literature from the University of South Carolina and her master's degree in cinema studies from New York University. She has written a wide range of books for young people. When she is not researching or writing, she enjoys going to movies, practicing yoga, and spending time with her husband, daughter, and golden retriever. She lives in New York.